Our Natural World

The Earth We Live On

Trevor Terry & Margaret Linton

illustrated by
Duncan Smith

SIMON & SCHUSTER
YOUNG BOOKS

Contents

Commissioning editor: Daphne Butler
Design: David Bennett Books
Illustration: Duncan Smith

First published in Great Britain 1992
by Simon and Schuster Young Books

Simon and Schuster Young Books
CAMPUS 400, Maylands Avenue
Hemel Hempstead, Herts, HP2 7EZ

Printed and bound in Great Britain
by BPCC Hazell Books
Paulton and Aylesbury

A catalogue record of this book is available
from the British Library
ISBN 0 7500 0838 5

Our World

The world we live on is called the Earth. On the Earth there are seas and rivers, mountains and deserts, grasslands and forests.

People live all over the world.

The place where you live is only a very tiny part of the Earth.

This picture shows how the Earth looks from a spaceship. Astronauts in space can see that the Earth is shaped like a ball. They can see sea and clouds, and land as well.

A globe is shaped like a ball and shows a map of the whole Earth. It shows us the oceans and seas, and the shape of the land.

Going round the sun

The Earth is a planet. Planets are worlds that travel round a sun. The path that a planet takes around a sun is called its orbit.

Nine planets have orbits round our sun. Our sun and its planets are called the Solar System.

sun

Mars

Saturn

Venus

Mercury

Earth

Jupiter

Uranus

The planets take different times to orbit the sun. The Earth takes 1 year, Uranus takes 84 years, and Pluto takes nearly 250 years.

Some planets are smaller than the Earth, and some are very much bigger. Jupiter, the biggest, is about 11 times wider than the Earth.

Mercury is the nearest to the sun and it is very hot. Pluto is the furthest away and it is very cold.

As the Earth orbits the sun, it spins round and round.
It spins round once every 24 hours.

When the sun shines on one side of the Earth, it is daytime there.
The other side is then in darkness and it is night-time.

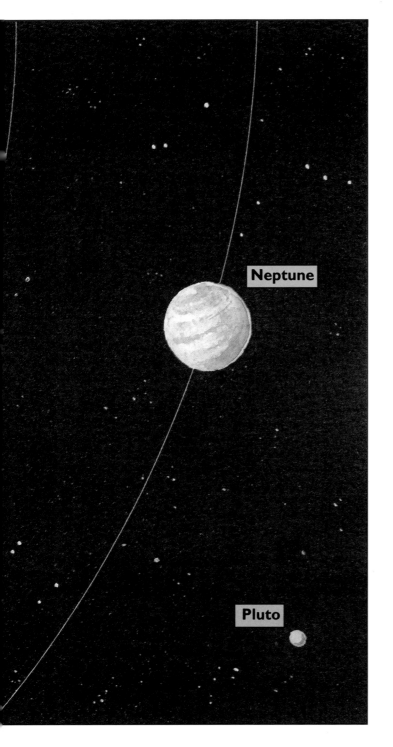

As the Earth spins round,
night slowly turns into day.
We call this dawn.
When day is turning into
night, we call it evening.

daytime   **night-time**

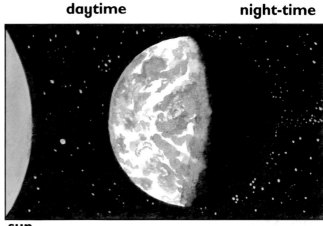

sun

As far as we know, there is
no life on the other planets
in the Solar System. Because
the Earth has air and water,
and it is neither too hot nor too
cold, plants and animals
can live here.

Earth is a very special place.

Inside the Earth

We think that the Earth began as a whirling cloud of gas and dust. As it slowly became more solid, three layers were formed. The outer layer, or crust, is the ground under our feet. The middle layer, or mantle, makes up most of the Earth. The inner layer is called the core. The mantle and the core are both very hot.

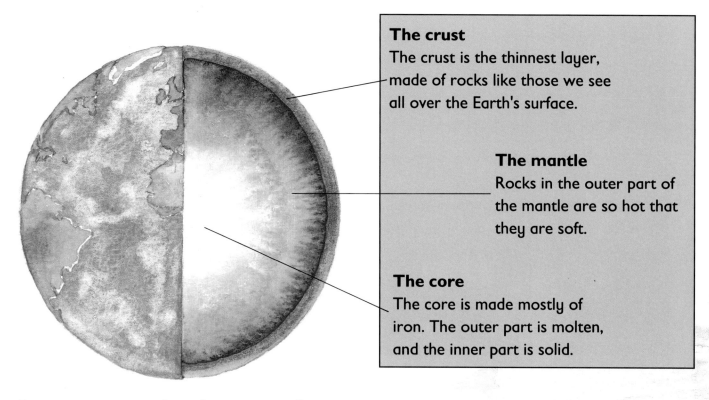

The crust
The crust is the thinnest layer, made of rocks like those we see all over the Earth's surface.

The mantle
Rocks in the outer part of the mantle are so hot that they are soft.

The core
The core is made mostly of iron. The outer part is molten, and the inner part is solid.

In some countries there are places where underground water is heated by hot rock. Hot water and steam spurt from holes in the ground. This is called a geyser.

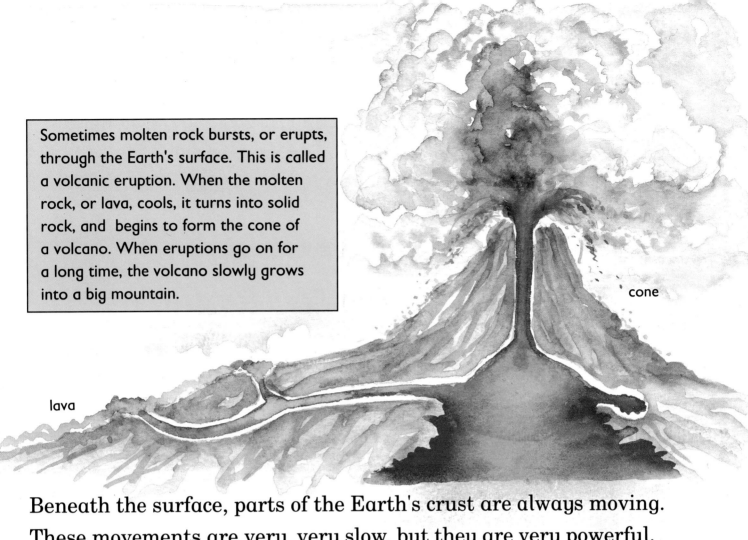

Sometimes molten rock bursts, or erupts, through the Earth's surface. This is called a volcanic eruption. When the molten rock, or lava, cools, it turns into solid rock, and begins to form the cone of a volcano. When eruptions go on for a long time, the volcano slowly grows into a big mountain.

cone

lava

Beneath the surface, parts of the Earth's crust are always moving. These movements are very, very slow, but they are very powerful.

Movement beneath the Earth's surface, has caused mountains to be pushed up, both on land and under the sea.

Sometimes parts of the Earth's crust suddenly move against each other. The ground shakes and cracks. Earthquakes cause a lot of damage.

7

Oceans and continents

Nearly three-quarters of the Earth's surface is covered by water, and nearly all the water is salty. There are six vast areas of salty water which we call oceans.

The oceans are all joined together, and stretch right round the Earth.

The map shows six oceans:

1. Arctic Ocean
2. North Atlantic Ocean
3. South Atlantic Ocean
4. Pacific Ocean
5. Indian Ocean
6. Southern Ocean

The Pacific Ocean is the largest and deepest.

The Arctic Ocean is the smallest and is not as deep as the others.

Some parts of the oceans near to land are called seas.

The map also shows seven continents.

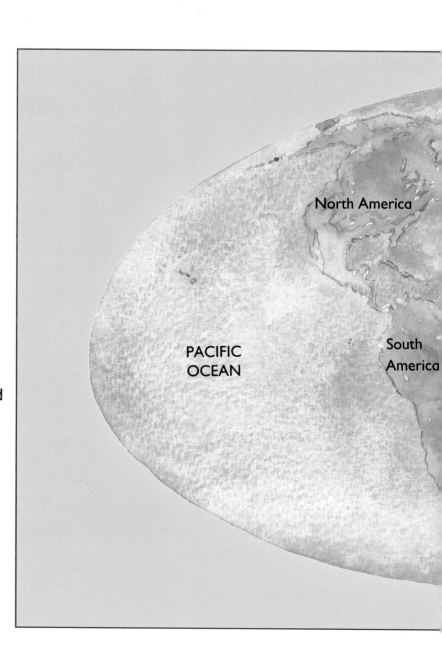

At the bottom of the oceans there are flat plains and high mountains. The tops of some mountains are above the surface of the oceans and they form islands.

Between the oceans there are huge areas of land called continents. Look at the map. Find the continents of Africa, Australasia, Asia, Antarctica, North and South America, and Europe.

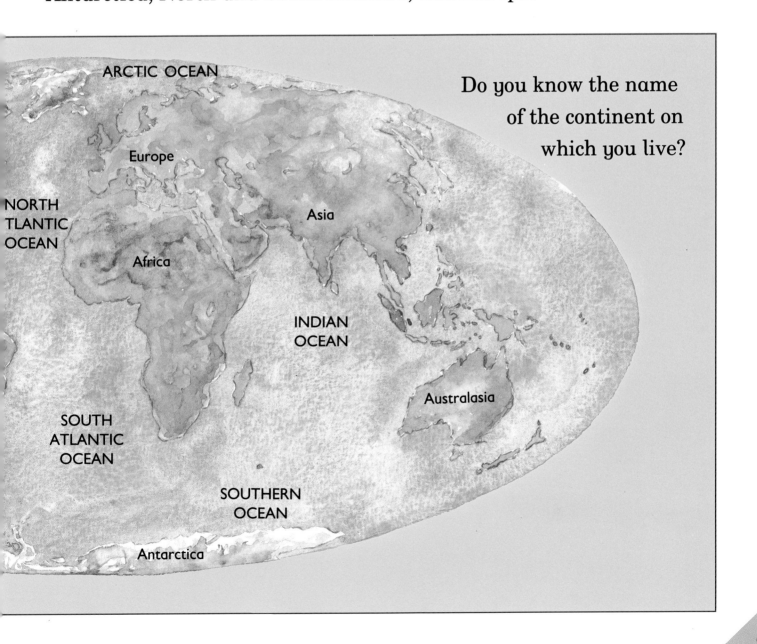

ARCTIC OCEAN

Do you know the name of the continent on which you live?

Europe

NORTH
TLANTIC
OCEAN

Asia

Africa

INDIAN
OCEAN

Australasia

SOUTH
ATLANTIC
OCEAN

SOUTHERN
OCEAN

Antarctica

The sea is never still. On the surface, there are waves caused by the wind. Below the surface, there are currents of water that flow from place to place. One current, called the Gulf Stream, carries warm water across the Atlantic Ocean to northern Europe. It makes winter warmer there.

Most fish live in seas close to continents. The seas are not as deep as the oceans beyond.

fishing boat

Strong winds, blowing across a sandy shore, can build sand up into dunes.

sand dune

The shore is where the sea meets the land. Shores may be rocky, pebbly, sandy or muddy. Where the land is high above the sea, it ends in cliffs. Twice each day, the sea rises and falls. This is called the tide.
As the tide rises, the sea comes in and covers the shore. Later, when the tide falls, the sea goes out again.

cliff

When waves break against cliffs they slowly wear them away.

Groynes are needed to stop sand and pebbles from being washed away.

groyne

Sea walls are built to stop towns and villages from being flooded.

The land

On land there are hills and high mountains, and also wide open spaces. There are places where trees cover the ground, and others where it is too cold for any plants to grow. Some places are wet and marshy, and some are dry and sandy. The pictures show what some of these places look like.

Mountains

Swamp

Grassland

Desert

Rainforest

Frozen waste

Rocks

The surface of the Earth is made of rock. In some places we can see the rocky surface, but in most places it is covered with soil. We see bare rock on mountains and cliffs, and in places where it juts out of the ground.

There are many kinds of rock. Here are a few.

granite

sandstone

shale

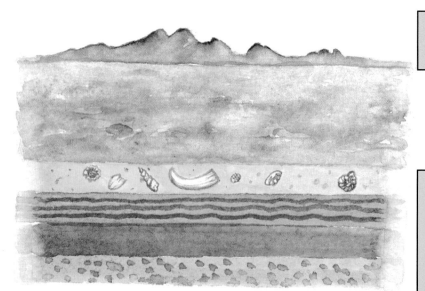

Some rocks, like granite, were formed from molten rock inside the Earth.

Others, like sandstone and shale, were formed at the bottom of the sea. Grains of sand and mud, as well as the skeletons and shells of animals, sank to the bottom of the sea. There they slowly changed into solid rock.

In some rocks like limestone, we often find fossils of animals. These animals were living when the rocks were being formed under the sea.

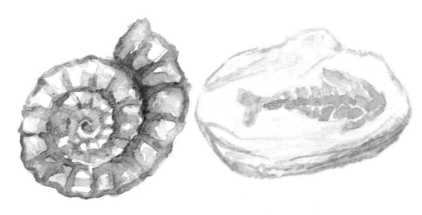

Rocks are broken into smaller pieces by water as it freezes.
Pebbles on beaches are pieces of rock worn smooth by the waves.

Wind and rain wear away rocks. Sometimes they are worn into strange shapes.

As rocks wear away, tiny grains fall to the ground. When they are mixed with tiny pieces of decayed plants and animals, soil is made. Plants need soil to grow in, and we need plants for food.

The Earth's atmosphere

Around the Earth is a layer of air called the atmosphere. We need the atmosphere to stay alive. Our bodies use the air which we breathe all the time. The atmosphere protects our bodies from harmful rays from the sun. It stops the Earth from getting too hot by day and too cold by night.

In the air there are different gases. One of these gases is called oxygen. Our bodies need oxygen to give us the energy to do things.

As we go higher and higher, there is less and less air. It gets harder and harder to breathe. Climbers on high mountains take oxygen with them. They carry the oxygen in special containers.

The higher we go, the colder it gets. Climbers need warm clothing.

Beyond the atmosphere is space. In space it is always dark. When the sun shines through our atmosphere, the sky above us looks blue. There is water in the atmosphere which we cannot see. It is called water vapour. Moving air in the atmosphere is called wind. Our weather happens in the atmosphere.

When water vapour in the atmosphere cools, it turns into clouds and rain. When it is very cold, drops of water in the clouds freeze and join together to become snowflakes.

Sometimes the wind in the atmosphere travels very fast. Then we have gales and hurricanes.

In hot weather warm air rises up into the sky. When this warm air meets the colder air above, storm clouds are formed, and there is thunder and lightning.

Seasons of the year

There are four seasons in the year, each with its own kind of weather. The seasons are called summer, autumn, winter and spring.

Summer
Summer is the warmest season, and the days are long. The sun rises early in the morning and sets late in the evening.

Autumn
Autumn is the season when summer is turning into winter. The weather becomes colder and the days become shorter.

Spring
Spring is the season when winter is turning into summer. The weather becomes warmer and the days become longer.

Winter
Winter is the coldest season, and the days are short. The sun rises later in the morning and sets earlier in the evening.

The seasons change as the Earth orbits the sun.
They change because the Earth leans to one side.
We say that the Earth is tilted.

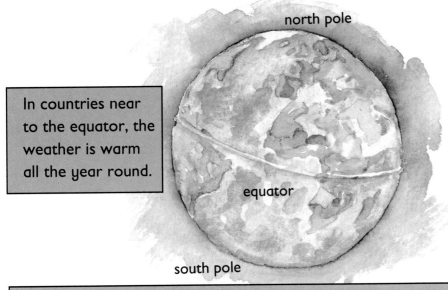

north pole

equator

south pole

In countries near to the equator, the weather is warm all the year round.

At the north and south poles, the weather is very cold. There is always snow and ice there.

In June, the northern half of the Earth is tilted towards the sun, and in December, the southern half is. The half tilted towards the sun gets more sunshine, and it is summer there. The half tilted away from the sun gets less sunshine and it is winter. Spring and autumn are the times in-between.

Each day aeroplanes fly from one half of the Earth to the other.
One day you could be in summer and the next in deepest winter.

19

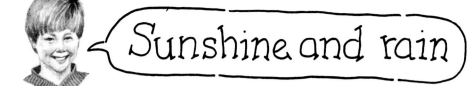

If you look up into the sky on a clear night, you will see the stars. Each star is a sun. The nearest star to the Earth is our sun.

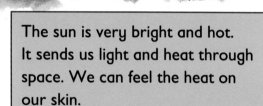

The sun is very bright and hot. It sends us light and heat through space. We can feel the heat on our skin.

In the picture, the children's bodies have stopped the light from reaching the sand on the beach. That is how shadows are formed.

Never look straight at the sun. The strong light can damage your eyes.

Plants need the light and warmth of the sunshine to make them grow.

Some days are cloudy and you can't see the sun. Remember that above the clouds the sun is always shining.

Clouds are made of tiny drops of water. Sometimes the drops join together and make raindrops. Raindrops fall to the ground as rain.

Sometimes before the rain stops, the sun comes out. When this happens you might see a rainbow. To see a rainbow the sun must be behind you. The sun shines on the raindrops and the sunlight is split up into different colours.

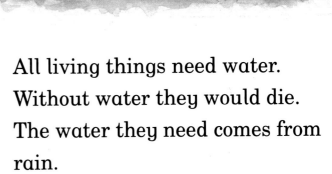

All living things need water. Without water they would die. The water they need comes from rain.

Streams and rivers

stream

waterfall

reservoir

Water in streams and rivers comes from rain, and sometimes from melting snow as well.

Stream

Streams are often clear and fast flowing. Rushing water wears away rocks, and makes steep banks. It carries sand and stones downstream.

Waterfall

When a stream or river flows over the edge of a cliff it makes a waterfall. The water drops into a pool below.

Reservoir

A reservoir is a place where water is stored. A dam is built across a valley to hold water from streams and rivers.

The place where a river begins is called its source. A river grows bigger as water from small streams drains into it. Other rivers may join the main river before it reaches the sea. These are called tributaries. The place where a river flows into the sea is called an estuary.

river   marshes   estuary

River

A river is a wide stream. Some rivers are very wide and flow slowly. Many kinds of plants and animals may live there.

Marshes

Marshes are wet places and rivers often flood them in winter. Grass grows well, and farm animals feed there in summer.

Estuary

An estuary is where fresh water from a river meets the salt water of the sea. Ships sail into ports, which are often built on estuaries.

Exploring places

Long ago people set out in sailing ships from the land they knew. They discovered new countries and met new people whose lives were different to their own.

Today, we are beginning to explore space. Astronauts have visited the surface of the moon. They didn't find any living things, but they brought back some pieces of rock.

We send satellites and space probes into space.

Earth

Mars

Satellites send us pictures of the Earth. The pictures tell us about the weather and how the Earth is changing.

Space probes send us pictures of other planets. These pictures tell us what the land and atmosphere are like.

We use satellites and space probes to explore for us.

People also explore for adventure.

Some people explore under the ground. They climb down into dark caves and passages.

stalactites

stalagmites

Caves are made by underground rivers. Water slowly wears away the rocks. Some rocks have strange shapes. Stalactites hang from the roofs of caves. Stalagmites grow up from the floors.

Some people explore under the sea. They dive down to look for the creatures that live there. Divers wear special clothes. They take their air with them, so that they can breathe under the water.

Exploration helps us to learn more about our world and space.

Using the land

We live on the land and we use it in different ways.

We use it for farming.

We need land for growing food
for ourselves and animals, and
for growing trees.

We use it for building.

Some people live in small villages.

Other people live in large towns and cities.

We use it for travel.

Roads, railways and airports use up a lot of land. We need them so that we can travel about.

We use it for enjoyment.

Grown ups and children both enjoy outdoor activities. When we are out of doors we enjoy seeing wildlife all around us.

Hidden treasure

For a long time people have been digging down into the Earth's rocky surface.

They have dug pits and quarries for stone, chalk, clay, and small stones called gravel. They have used these for building.

Stone quarry

bricks and tiles (made from clay)

stone wall

concrete (cement mixed with sand, gravel and water)

glass (made from sand, limestone and soda)

cement (clay mixed with chalk or limestone)

copper (used for water pipes and electric wire inside the house)

They have mined for rocks called ores. These rocks contain minerals which can be made into metals like iron and copper.

copper ore

People have dug deep mines to find precious things like gemstones and gold. Gemstones which are used for jewellery must be cut and polished.

sapphire gemstone

gold ring with sapphire and diamond gemstones

People also mine for coal.

Millions of years ago giant plants fell down into swamps and were covered by mud and sand. The plants decayed and were squashed by the layers of rock above. Slowly the decayed plants turned into coal.

Coal mine

People have drilled deep wells to find gas and oil.

Oil well

Gas and oil formed from the remains of tiny sea plants and animals that lived millions of years ago.

Oil is used to make petrol, plastics and many other things. We use gas for heating and cooking.

oil trapped between layers of rocks

We must keep the air clean.

We must look after

We should try to
keep our streets
clean and tidy.

We must look after trees and forests.

It's our world.

30

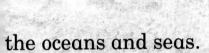
the oceans and seas.

We must keep streams and rivers clean.

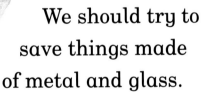

We should try to save things made of metal and glass.

We must look after the land we farm.

We must take care of it.

Index